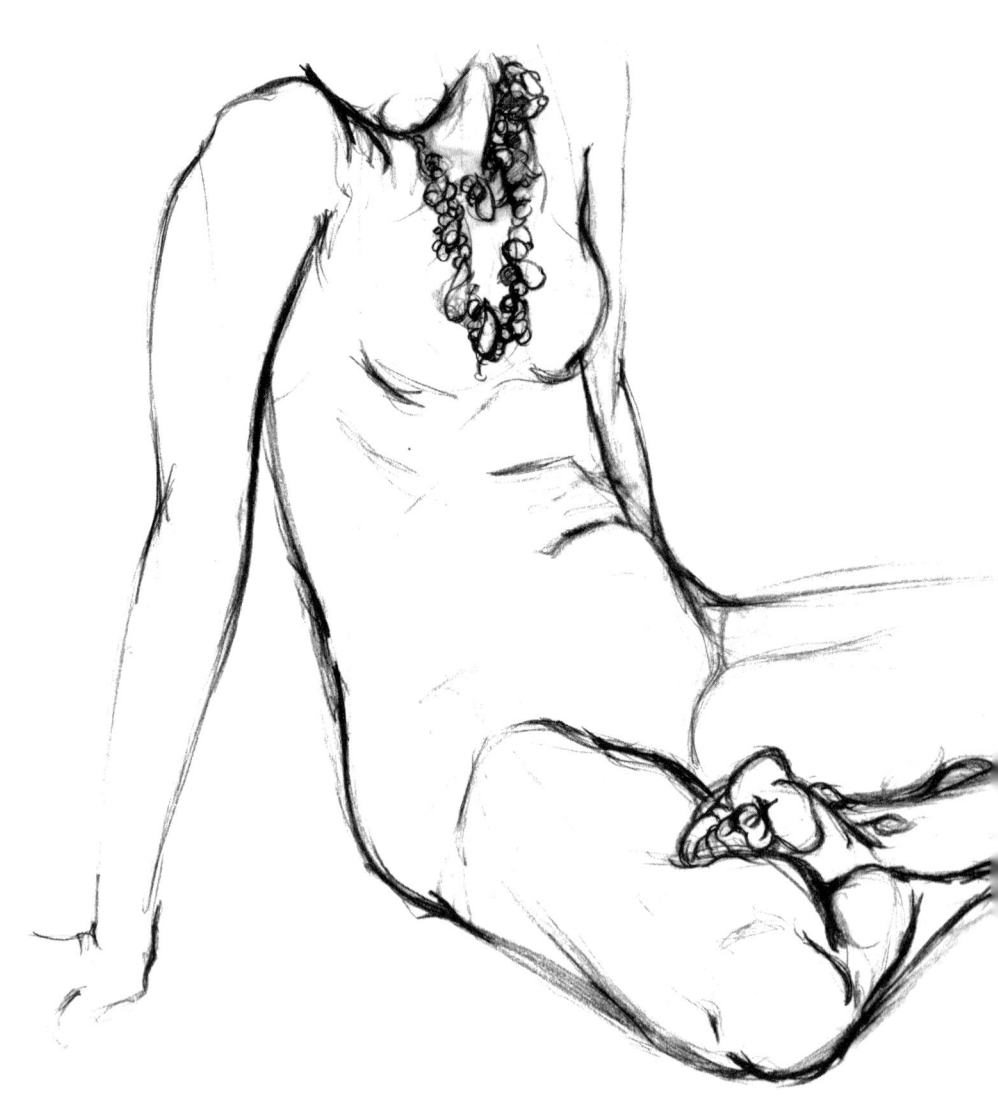

THIS BODY SHE'S ENTERED

Poems by
Mary Kay Rummel

with drawings by
Sandra Rummel

Minnesota Voices Project Number 41
NEW RIVERS PRESS

Copyright ©1989 by Mary Kay Rummel
All rights reserved
Library of Congress Catalog Card Number: 89-62212.
ISBN 0-89823-115-9.
Author photo by Steve Krumm
Typesetting and Book Design by Peregrine Publications
Edited by Vivian Vie Balfour

The author wishes to express her grateful acknowledgement to the following publications in which some of these poems, in slightly different form, first appeared: *Sing Heavenly Muse; Onionskin; Loonfeather; Lake Street Review; Primavera; Visions; Northeast; Abraxas; Milkweed Chronicle; Contemporary Review; Whittier Globe; A Change in Weather: Midwest Women Poets; Saturday's Women Anthology; Full Circle Two;* and *Harbinger*.

The author wishes to thank the following individuals for their kind attention to *This Body She's Entered* in manuscript: Pat Barone, Sharon Chmielarz, Norita Dittburner-Jax, Carol Masters, Laura Littleford, Deborah Keenan, Vivian Vie Balfour, and Bill Truesdale.

This Body She's Entered has been published with the aid of grants from the Jerome Foundation, the First Bank System Foundation, the Arts Development Fund of the United Arts Council, and the National Endowment for the Arts (with funds appropriated by the Congress of the United States). We also wish to thank the Minnesota Non-Profits Assistance Fund for its invaluable support.

New Rivers Press books are distributed by

> The Talman Company
> 150-5th Avenue
> New York, NY 10011

The Body She's Entered has been manufactured in the United States of America for New Rivers Press (C. W. Truesdale, Editor/Publisher) 420 N. 5th St., Suite 910, Minneapolis, MN 55401 in a first edition of 1,200 copies.

Above Them Both

1 SHE WORE MY MOTHER'S FACE

3 Seamstress
4 White Haired Woman
5 An Autumn of Hands
6 Hunting for Ghosts
9 The Catch
11 Step on a Crack
14 Fat Nun on Fat Tuesday
15 Homecoming: Skye, Scotland
16 The Nun Speaks in Church

2 BODY AND SOUL ARE ONE

21 This Is Our Inheritance
23 Five Sisters Window: York
24 Rage Journal
28 *De Profundis*
29 Eye to Eye
30 Letter to a Former Mother Superior
31 Renaissance
33 Talking with a Window
35 How One Leaves the Order

3 THIS MATTER OF SKIN

43 Triptych
45 Fishing Is What We Go On Doing
48 How the Cold Comes
51 Still Photography
52 Let the Dead Bury the Dead
55 Water
56 Cambridge, England 1986
57 From Each Hand
58 Of Circles and My Sons
60 Oh Yes We Have Been Here Before: Stratford
61 In the North
62 Letter from a Downtown Hotel
63 White Herons
64 Gifts for a Birthday
65 Growing Older

67 Biographical Note

*This book is dedicated to Tim,
Timothy, Andy, and
all my teachers*

Above Them Both

I am painting my wall.
Let the mother have a corner
the one who sits
outside the hut
preparing corn and beans for cooking.
Her children run in and out of her mouth
protected
sent out
protected again.

Let the nun have a corner
the last in the long line
of black robed women
who brought me to this time.
Because I absorbed their prayers
because I grew their chants for feet
because their hungers
carved the caves
of my stone face
I grew curved
with a cup for a belly.

Above them both
I paint the loon
all arrowhead and feathers
slivered moons on black wings
shot from the water's bow.

Today I straighten to fly
on new found winds.

1
SHE WORE MY MOTHER'S FACE

*...and you knew that you
stood on the brink of that sea that was
neither charted nor plumbed by men, that
sea-shore only women had known, dark with
its sailing red lights of storms, where only the
feet of women had trod, hearing the thunder
of the sea in their ears as they gathered the
fruit on that waste, wild shore...*

from A Scots Quair *by* Lewis Gibbon

Seamstress

I remember a sewing machine
a black Singer with a pedal
that tapped all afternoon
beneath my grandmother's foot.
Her thick fingers pushed cotton
and silk into its snapping mouth
until her eyes darkened from strain.
Parades of bright dresses,
shirts, shawls tumbled from her machine.
On our thin bodies
we wore her eyes.

In the mirror
I see my mother's face
and my grandmother's face
a long parade of Irish Marys
with tunnels for eyes
holes where children crawl
eyes made blind
from too much looking
at the sea.

Afternoons
I feed my typewriter
raw fear and strange words
the cotton pieces of my life.
They step out whole
and walk away on thin legs
solid like mirrors
with eyes wide open.

White Haired Women

world that says simply
snow

outside my door
runs the white river
pounds the white sea
we drown in wave after wave

I watch the slow drift
from behind glass
daughter of shore watchers

daughter of white haired women
I love and am afraid of loving

see them
on windy street corners
scarves anchor their chins

see them
come straight from the hair dressers
curls hugging their heads

they come from old islands
to this snow
white with blue shadows

An Autumn of Hands

I look to the river for answers
but the river
is losing its voice.
I listen instead to my hands
that are wells.
In them my own eyes sing.

My hands
drive like moles through layers
and layers of things
to be accomplished.
Something in me wants to break apart
have all dead ends stripped away
be absolute
fundamental.

I watch my mother pick petunias
from a browning plant.
She closes her eyes
for a moment
her whole life
dies in her hands.

Hunting for Ghosts

Old Tapestry (Ghost of Solitude)

The unicorn could leap the small fence
but he stays in his warm country
surrounded by leaves (which are foods)
and blazing fruit (which is sex).
His voice was a river in a lush green valley
but I left him for the snow plains
of my childhood. My ghosts speak
only when I'm alone.

Talking (Ghost of Silence)

There is nothing the matter with words
just because they are hidden from me.
There is nothing the matter
with crows or empty oaks.
It is my loneliness not theirs.
I try to find words
for the exact handling of distance.

Collecting

The sea stones we gathered
are bleached to bone.
Where I live the sky is filled with them.
I open my shades to their cold claims.

To See a Face (Ghosts of Dreams and Childhood)

Who are these women
who haunt my dreams
who won't let me touch myself
or let a man in me?
Their faces are the same onion.
Their shrill voices shriek
from the bedposts.

Somehow we must
draft a treaty.
I agree to acknowledge
even love them.
I don't cross the street
when I see them walking
out of my past.
We pass in front of the ice cream store.
I smile, "Good morning, Sisters,"
and look for some wisdom in their eyes.

London (Ghost of Loneliness)

Forgotten by windows
I looked into afternoons.
Leaned against other peoples' roses
Disguised as rain.

Edinburgh (Ghost of Memory)

The spiral staircase cuts
through layers of history
to this ancient street.
I know the garden
of the silent lady
with pulled back hair.
I hope you just visit here, O lady,
that you live in a kingdom of air.
Lady of memory of forgetting
you carry my name scratched
in stone.

On the Chair (Ghost in the Wind)

Like a crooked tree I wait
for the wind that blows only here.
Ghost woman in the upstairs room.
She in the shadows is quiet is hungry.
She is old but her breasts are young.
Her nipples remember his tongue.
Her hands still love his hair.
When we make love she laughs softly.

Forgiving

The doors in my fingers
and toes are open.
The sign says,
"Please remove your clothes."
I am tired.
do you ever just want to touch
skin again?
My skin wearing yours
the whole hard length of it.

Ghost Closest

most distant
mother father
friend lover
self

The Catch

   1
I fish casting many lines
into wind, into water.
I try not to snag the large weeds
to avoid the stretch and break.
Mother   lover   daughter
Is there anything beneath this surface
besides my own face?

   2
I stared for hours at mobiles of light
in streams and lakes just waiting
for god to appear. Now I know I saw her
and she wore my face and my mother's face.

   3
Mother, you stood in a morning boat
a shadow in the grey meeting of water and sky
a long dark bolt the door of the moment opened
swinging into a tomorrow you could have entered.
But you stayed loving the small bay
the larger lake behind it. Loving the waiting
the lines you couldn't see in the mist
the connection that would tell you it was worth it.

   4
When I go fishing I take children.
Instead of catching fish I untangle lines
hook worms and pass pop.
Once six children's lines tangled underwater.
They struggled together, earthworms strangling
each other beneath the mud. Sometimes we did too.

5
Mother you told me
of my grandmother on the boat from Ireland
how it was so stormy she thought she would die.
After that she was afraid of water.
She prayed the rosary in boats
never let you swim. You made me
afraid of death by water.
You wore it in fingers always knotting.
In nightmares I always lose my loves in water.

6
Your death is worse than death by drowning.

You have your suitcase packed and are ready
to give birth to it. Your fingers
no longer knot. You are dying
but I feel I am.
My shore is shifting
a line drawn to make me safe.
I can't pull down the shades of bone.
With only the wind for clothing
we die over and over.
I am the mother. I am the child.

7
I want you to stay
poised in that borderless place
where past and present run blind.
I watch you decide to leave
held by trembling lines that tug you back
and I tell you to break free.
You swim toward a new country
looking for the light.

Step on a Crack

Meditation on a line from Haunted by the Holy Ghost, *a play by Jan MaGrane:*
"I don't want to be like you; I want to be holy."

Young girl:
I don't want
    "step on a crack
    and you'll break
    your mother's back"
    a voice warns in her mind
I don't want to make you angry.
But I don't want to be
    a mother of boys
    a cleaner
    a cook.
I don't want to be like
    the white haired women
    in house dresses.
I don't want a double chin.
I don't want to lose a breast.
I don't want to be like you
    you serve my dad and brothers.
I don't want to be like you
    who cares about me.
I want to be like
    Joan, Virgin and Soldier
    Teresa, Virgin and Scholar
    Maria, Virgin and Martyr
those women who really knew how to suffer.

Her Mother: (years later)

Daughter,
we have fought our way to this
    the beds you wouldn't make
    the jobs you wouldn't take
    the men you wouldn't date
because you didn't want to be like me.
And here you are with me again
in the place you left.
You telling me that now you know
I was always holy and strong
honest about my scars.
I'm afraid of you now.
I won't let you touch them.

Daughter: (Somewhat older)

Mother,
I dream you walk away from me
to a womb-like place where crowds
have gone before you.
Such grieving, raging crowds
like the TV faces at foreign funerals.
I think you will be trampled by them.
You grow tinier.
I can't see my mother in you
I see my child.
As you get close to the place
you walk taller and disappear
with the straightening.

You couldn't teach me how to be
the woman I chose
but you show me how to be old
how to choose life when dying
looks easier
that something in us grows
taller as our bodies shrink.

Mother:

Through all this, Daughter
let's touch and hold now
when there is little time
for holding.
We will be like moose that rise
clean, as black water rolls
from their sides.
They become the strong dark
center of the harsh morning.

Fat Nun on Fat Tuesday

You writhe in front of us
in an almost sensual ecstacy
telling us to begin the fast.
It should hurt you say we should be hungry.
You need to inflict some pain
on your own flesh.
You say it won't kill us its the mirror
we shrink from.

As if the pain drifting back
from our own deaths wasn't enough.
As if the letting go didn't sing
like a bird over our hot sleeping bodies
bodies that will not be easily discarded.
As if it were not something large
like the deep wind or sea large enough
to hold us become suddenly small.
As if its true power is no more
that the lost sweet juice of an orange
or of love.

Homecoming: Skye, Scotland

I stand on rocks
on stone
sea eyes of Celtic women I
sway above the churning past

in me
the chain of Celtic women martyrs broken
a chain of women forged by waves
cold   wind   vile gods
child bearing bodies

yet in this place
my mothers and I keen together
their shadows whisper
in me

I have lived by this sea
all my lives
but will no more

The Nun Speaks in Church

She tells us to love the earth,
that we are made of star dust
grown from the evolution of flowers.
"How do you feel about the earth?"
she asks and I laugh.
They are her age now, some older,
the nuns who taught me to abandon the world,
to renounce my own young face.

"I don't miss sex," a nun told me
"because I've never experienced it."
In my dreams they watch me make love
and laugh behind their long white fingers.
"The shadow is under the bed," they say.
"Sad renter on earth.
You will be evicted soon."

They taught me to give up the earth
before it could abandon me
to turn away from sea wind
and remain a thin black etching
in the flattened snows
of my childhood.

Each night I renounce my body.
Forget how my fingers sing
a man's flesh between them.
Deny the slow ceremonies
opening, entering filling.
I start with my toes
work upwards towards my heart.

But morning arrives
with its dark gift of coffee.
Even in winter a bird sings.
The tattered tree outside my window
holds the sunrise in its heart
as I take my body back.

2
BODY AND SOUL ARE ONE

this is a cold
country
here you believe
in flesh

the cold
reminds you

    Siv Cedering

This is Our Inheritance

> *"When female nature, naturally so perverse, becomes sublime through holiness, it can be the noblest vehicle of grace."* a monk in The Name of the Rose
> by Umberto Eco

All over Europe
on last jugdement portals
of medieval cathedrals,
lust with its grinning belly and ass's head
carries nude women off to damnation,
faceless women slung over his shoulder
their hair hanging long.

On the left side of the main portal
of Chartres Cathedral
place of the lost, the damned
one woman walks, is not carried,
is not faceless, a nun,
all but her face covered.

And she smiles as she walks
a message to generations of us
necksore women.

"It was worth it," she says,
"Like nothing that ever happened before."

    "I love to look at you," he said,
    "to talk while I am loving you."

"I had closed my body for a long cold season.
In one brief transit I opened for him."

    "You smell so good to me," he said.
    "I love to taste you."

"He loved my body.
With him my body was my soul.
He imprinted it."

    "I love to listen
    to your small sounds."

"I wanted to swallow him
in me, one heliacal rising."

On her knees in the cold mornings
she tried to exorcise him.
In the night when she beat her flesh
his face grew on her thighs.

"In this city of God
built by men whom should I ask
for forgiveness?
In this book of glass
written by men
in their circular summing up
a yearly spiral opening inward
where do I who have broken out
come back to the same death?
These circles that open into God
close down on a woman who knows
that body and soul are one."

Five Sisters Window: York

(to women who grew up Roman Catholic)

we are of the time before this church
the time after this church
but not of this church
we are sisters
like the window in York cathedral
rose window mosiac of light
earth grey and stabbed with fire
our music swallowed by sacred space
an old silence in our ears

this child of ours
is grown larger that we are
turned terror and tyrant
we know its shadows well
    they are the nuns
      who lurk in our dream worlds
      taking on the forms of men we love
every building we choose to visit
becomes a monastery

Rage Journal

> *"How sweet the bells ring now the nuns are dead."*
> Helen Adams

1
Of Red Earth

The morning runs thick with strawberries
the irregular thump of berries against a box.
Women move down the rows like red spiders
arms, legs everywhere.
One tells the story
of a man who seduced her
while his wife slept in the back seat
and they giggle embarrassed
that they have been taught to hate it
that they have been taught to like it.
And the berries hide deep under thick vines
irresistibly wet and red.
They flash warm images of pie and jam
signs that say, "Take me."
The women crouch low
lost in red thoughts
and find them.

2
Of Red Water

That first convent day she put on black clothes
and noticed the lipstick, bright red lipstick
slashed across white skin made whiter by black veils.
none of the girls wanted to wash it off.
They would soon enough be pale logs claimed by waves
then thrown ashore and bleached bone dry.

It was an ancient buffeting they stepped into
and over it all a red cast as when certain parts
of the lake bare a deep red color
separated from surrounding blue
some recurring violence,
blood ever mixed with water in eternal menstruation.

Saturday nights they were given tiny chains
"de profundis clamavi ad te domine"
out of the depths they cried.
Chanters lined up in dark corridors:
the beat regular
in that dark
hitting their skin
hate and love of flesh
twisted like the chains
that left red slashes
on soft white thighs.

"Beware of smegma," the old monsignor said.
He stood before them, white hair crowning
a long black robe.
"He must be holy," the girls thought,
as he told them of the smegma
that lay within their bodies
stirring up carefully ignored vaginas.
"Take a shower," he said, "a cool shower."
They listened and squirmed
warm in their visions of smegma
red, wet, and new found.

3
Of Rock

For her
home was a place
to be without wanting
but she had no home
her mother her sisters
gave her the wrong directions
they said it was with a god.

The priests had a mahogany dining room
a long table and glass topped buffet.
Being poised and smart she served them
juice glasses from right
remove plates from left
smile but don't talk.
She listened they said
If you are poor you are rich
if you are sad you are happy
when you are dead you will be alive.

They took away the well of her voice
gave her back a cricket in cold air.
She touched the pews
traveled the roads within the wood
listening
but only the rocks were growing.

4
Of Clover

She knelt at the feet
of the stone nun,
immaculate like the song
"Immaculate Mary our hearts are on fire."
This woman's eyes burned with hatred
smoking like dry ice.

Looking like that,
the girl thought,
she has to be a mystic nun,
The Lady of the Garden
alabaster face frozen
in a half moon smile or grimace
on a permanent fast
belt hanging low on a missing waist.

She never raised her voice
or shoulders or eyes
as if she had forgotten the sky.
Her words bit like hard rain:

"In this garden, some of you girls are lilies,
some are roses, but you, my child, are clover."

I am clover, not stone
the girl thought.
In spring my milk will turn green.

de Profundis

with eyes full of space the apple tree dreams
of roots as giants' fingers
of branches as towers, strings of bridges
walled abbey town
fisted monks, foreheads on the damp floor
bet themselves with switches
in dark corridors they are half opened hands

you said you dug graves in the rain
graves for men you never knew
you chanted as you dug
the shovel rising falling
when I hear the chants I think of you
and of myself in the early morning
voice   body   a tree in the wind of those notes

a funeral started all this
and myself wanting to enjoy my body
guilt scrapes a dry leaf against a branch
I listen, go on to circle my breasts
at this moment of night they spin into blossom
you turn in your sleep temple
let me hold you
in my hands you will soften

outside the church feel it
a tingling
a let-down
a rain of milk
monks walk in line to breakfast
milk flows beneath their sandals
sunlight on wood milk and bees
each spring in the tree
an explosion of nipples

Eye to Eye

"I will take with me the emptiness of my hands what you do not have you find everywhere"
　　　　　　　　　　　　　　　　　　W.S. Merwin

all day the cries of the crippled blackbird
from the window well hammer at my ears
insistent as my own heartbeat those moments
I feel a stranger building a shell
around my eyes and ears
all day the blackbird drums
at the edge of my silence
the silence I carry
an egg in a pouch

at night the bird is quiet
folded like a velvet ribbon
on black tissue I dream
my head is bald wake up afraid
want to break things without
beginning without
end that are edgeless

I lift the bird out so light a canoe
carefully with gloves afraid of beak and disease
the undersides of oranges half buried snails

my sheets littered with matted feathers
on my pillow
bits of shell

Letter to a Former Mother Superior

in a drawer in the kitchen
onions kneel
circling their cut cords
in the parable
the man puts time in a bank
then grows so aware of seconds passing
the earth begins to spin beneath him
he lies on a couch and counts
insects thick in the air
the flies the nuns
folded in upon themselves

dear mother and sisters
I must confess
last week I broke silence
fifteen hundred times
and I still break it
smash it like a coffee cup
the brown eye of silence
stares from the floor

I walk to a stage
to give a poetry reading
look up to find the eyes of my friends
the audience is all nuns
white faces folded in stiff wings
eyes   beards
they come to claim me
these tellers of silence

Renaissance:
words From the Old One Within

for Linda Gregg

I am visiting a convent,
an old Spanish chapel.
On the altar three young women read
no, not read, but let the words flow.
I want to be one of them.
What is left of my house is too little.

Tell the dream, Old Woman,
Tell this dream.

"The book is the moment
a river of poetry
the altar, your life.
You are the young women
and the one who watches.
You are the space
in the empty bell tower
wanting light."

In the soup kitchen
a man scribbles poems
on paper marked Catholic Charities.
"I write my own," he says
and passes out his poems to the old men
who see only the insides of their own heads.

"You don't know," she says,
"That the one who traces
the outlines of your face,
who says, 'you are lovely,'
is within you."

Sweeper of the broken evening
you leave blood in the snow of memory
rock the stairs within me
to the wheeling city of night.
Heavy song
you circle the trees with longing
stones dropped by the Old One
a trail to lead us home, blind.

And we write our poems
not knowing it is in this river
of language that we are healed
this passing out of the pages
of our lives.
As the men walk from the shelter
they hold a white bird
caged in their whipcord hands.

Tell this dream, Old Woman,
Tell this dream.

I am trapped inside monastery walls
a maze of hallways and cloisters
each with a different pattern
thick stone vaults above my head
and doors impossible to move.

"You are the altar and the women on it
the writer and the words
the light from within
in this time
when the bell light is missing.
You are the walls and the one who breaks
from the blind monastery of the mind."

Talking with a Window

(The Five Sisters Window in York Minster is dark glass stabbed by red slashes. It is figureless.)

If god appeared to me
what would she be like?

> "A womb."

Would she look like you
woman of the window
a black sea of roots that twist
over shafts of sapphire
scattered like poppies in a field?

> "And like you.
> Your unborn children
> cry to come out.
> The light sends them
> scurrying back inside."

Bless me, then, for I have sinned.

> "And I will bless you
> for you will sin again."

But I can't connect the two
the blessing and the sin.
I'm afraid of dying alone.
"You have ruined your life,"
scrawled on the walls of my room.

> "That's not god's voice.
> She's big enough, your god,
> for both, the blessing and the sin."

You mirror the sleeping dream in me
that sits up, shouts from my eyes.
The fearful church should camouflage
your spill of blood and longing.

> "It is your story I tell.
> Guard your own night.
> teeming and fragile as it is."

How One Leaves the Order

1
The Fantasy

It is the face
of water. One side
a still blue eye
the other a gray
thrashing.
Behind it all the swamp
where birches lose
their slim images.

When I look into water I see
my own face smooth
then broken again and again.
When I look into it I fall
my own shattered eyes
mending.

I lived once
in the swamp
tangled in roots
I had little knowing of,
explored that cloistered world,
swam dark corridors,
looking for doors long sealed,
forced my eyes to stay open long
after they wanted to close.
You may see me bright and calm,
but it is the dark lake
clean and wild
that I love.

2
The Ceremony

It happens in a boat on Whitefish Lake
as you and the loons watch the day end.
Beneath you the blue grey belly
of yesterday's rain.

You watch as if your life did not depend
on it. Watch as the sun screams from its isolated
point. It moves through spasms of color until
a blue veil carries it away. The loons wear
the straightness of night on their heads. They want
to fill it with their cries.

Then you know you carry your own grief. The cries
you hear in the night are yours. God
will never be grief to you again.

3
The Decision

it is flowing
down a river
that twists and slides
shadow into sunlight
into shadow

snag a rock
hesitate
then shove off again
hills and undersides of leaves
sway in the lean
and clouded light I float in
the currents
of my choice

summers
night in the north country
comes late
there is a silence
borne in the bodies
of trees that hover
between two worlds
as if they could choose
which to be in

I too hang
on that edge knowing
it is unnecessary
I carry my own night

   4
The Falling Back

Just when you figured you could do it
walk off the dock into clear water
get your hair wet say it straight out
you get caught again on the corner
of a word aimed at the heart and you begin
to struggle again.

Just when you figured you had it in you
you find that really isn't it at all.
Even here by the long limbed lake
it isn't the walking away that counts
it's the freedom to do it.

You are so wounded by god's silence. Arrow
in the chest missing the heart. Vital
organs are fine but there is danger
of infection. You just walk around
with it sticking out of both sides until someone
gets near enough to pull it out.

   5

The Feeling That You Carry It With You

Loons play wounded on the water
rise up with high pitched screams and fall
floating black humps in the vast lake.

They seem to say,
    "Come take us
    can't you see we're weak."
    I follow them in a wide course
    over the moon water
    then watch them shoot suddenly
    their bodies their cries upward
    black northbound arrows.

3
THIS MATTER OF SKIN

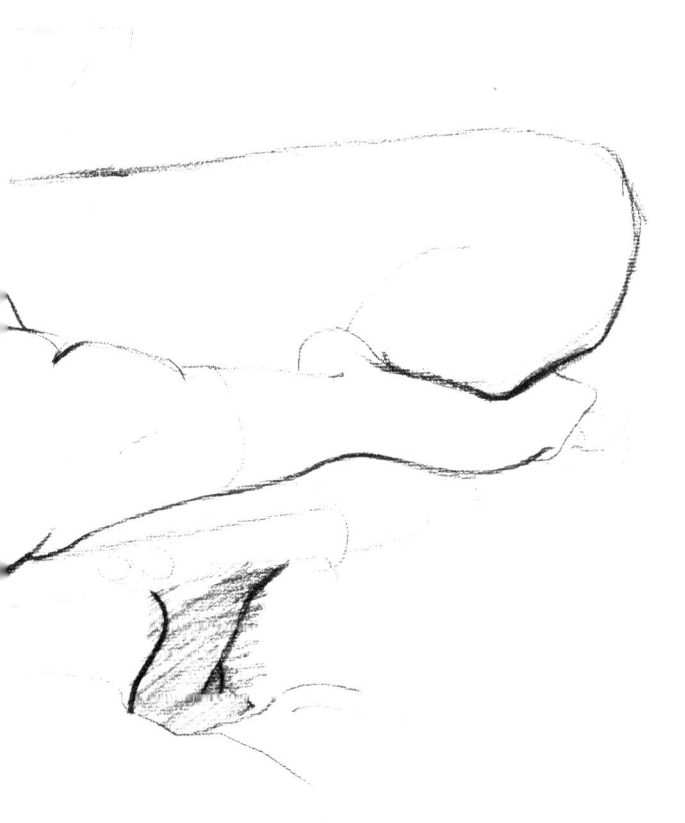

All my life I have wanted to touch your ankle
running down to its shore
I beach myself on you
I listen
I see you among still leaves

                    W.S. Merwin

Triptych

The past is the center.
An angel announces a baby.
From this, the lady must reclaim
her life each day.

In my past trees are nuns
who close oak doors
and burrow into white
knowing there will be no melt.
They meditate upon the virgin
not knowing abstinence is fear
of the angel and his announcements.

Today in the cloister gardens
their shadowless snow haunts us.
It softens the old arches.
Here stone and oleander love each other.
Chant lifts and swells a dry odor
of white and occasional color
pomegranite and lush green.
Its long fingers draw me backward
make me want to run.

Joseph peacefully carves wood
while outside his window
the town of the future widens
the crack in the heavy vision
of the medieval painter.
In front of them all
my eyes drink you and tell
the rest of my body how you taste.

You are my window, my love
a cityscape painted in the corner.
New feeling in an old place
binds the sections of my life.
When I leave my smell will stay
on your fingers fresh cut wood
left in the snow to dry.

Fishing is What We Go On Doing

"Was he married, did he try
to support as he grew less fond of them
wife and family?" Stevie Smith

On the edge of Derwentwater
the Englishman tells me of a Swedish friend
who returned from England
and went ice fishing
never stopping to see his wife and children.

I know that mania
as I walk the wide spaces of a frozen lake,
tread carefully through the village of men
where rimmed auger holes trip dogs and children.
Pastel fish houses lean together in the wind
and during the thaw cars slide easily under ice.

"It's okay about the wife," he says.
"But why not stop to see his children.
I believe in the innocence of children."

*

I know a man who lives in a bait shop
on the edge of ice. Men stop in at midnight
for minnows that splash in five tanks
or for leeches that grow in three sizes.
Jim welcomes each man, spreads his wide fingers
on their backs and sends them out. In sunlight
they return to describe the wanderings of fish
beneath their roofs of ice.

Jim looks at the frost and sees his wife
and daughters. His memory lifts off
the lovely shadows of their faces.
Then they step into air, no longer with him
in the wide lake light. Always large,
he has become strong like an oak.
He wraps what light there is around him
knowing he will not break.

*

The Englishman tells me about his father.
"He was an outdoorsman, a climber.
On Sundays when we hiked he marched ahead
leaving my mother with us children.
In midlife my father decided to do what he wanted.
He took his trips alone and all our outings stopped."

I listen, riveted by this man's green eyes
caught in a net of laugh lines.
"He is a man," I think, "who will never
leave his children." Suddenly the daughter
in me reaches out and touches my own distant father.
"My father never talked to us," I say,
"until my mother died."

He was the one I fished for,
dropping child hooks hoping he'd bite.
Now his forty years of silence
pile against the shore, jagged chunks,
ice stacked up and tumbling
one by one into the melt.

*

In the city Jim's wife remembers the lake,
thinks how she will go there on the weekend.
"It will do," she thinks, "for a winter morning."
Impatient and cautious, she remembers
how on certain mornings the light crept
around the drapes and filled the spaces
between the hairs on his chest.
"He will do," she thinks, "for a friend
or a lover." But not less. She won't have less.

*

It is the hills around Derwentwater
that give it mystery. Even in sunlight
they are shadowed by clouds of their own
like the faces of men who wait at a hole
for something to happen beneath ice.
They sit inside themselves, like trees, thinking.

How the Cold Comes

    1
autumn

this is the season of last beans
tough corn tumerous zucchini
at the market apples overflow their baskets
pinch our tongues   tease the frenzied bees

this is the season when water greys
the nights lose weight
the moon's a cutting edge
we disentangle   there is hurry
you roll over in bed
pull the blankets
and me with you
your back is a breakwater
but only our silence
punctuates the air
even gulls squabble at sunset
all night I hear the thud
of apples falling

    2
winter

how to tell you
that the lake means grief
to me now
those caves of winter
where we lost each other
I followed you then
hands on damp stone
feet in chill pools
was it a failure of language
unborn children
words that belonged with things
I would never touch again

here in these old bodies
we need to journey not war
I renounce predictions
but expect spring

    3

spring

my plants spilling out of their pots
do they know
without knowing
the fear of your leaving

it covers me at night
like a heavy net
I throw off and wake
calling your name

there is this matter of skin
between us
mounds
of old skin
each day's shedding
between us
skin in search of skin
even the sound of the violin
seems bound by skin that stretches

I am running swimming upstream
chasing fires in the forest
breaking through spider webs
over crushed leaves, broken
grass, fallen limbs
beneath my feet a path
I know nothing about
only the robin speaks
its mouth full of straw

    4

summer

among the olive greens
one yellowed tree
like the skulls monks keep
in front of their eyes
to remind them of death
when eating

I will now begin
to devour without guilt

I will hold in my hand
the frog cry "need"
gull cry "enough"

the oriole left a promise
on my lawn
two yellow feathers
spread thighs
black at the joining
I will devour
the lawn   the oriole
the thighs   the hair
the time of abstinence
is over

Still Photography

Try it out. Say you will never love again.
No future in it. That only pain waits
for you and you deserve it too.
Keep your body from sitting too long.
Don't give it a chance to remember
his hands on your breasts, you in the mirror
arched under his touch. Keep your heart
from singing those few times it wants to sing
because it loved him. Then change the dialogue.
Say you are destined to be loved. That you
deserve it. Say your skin wants to be touched.
Wrap his memory around you a story you try
to tell. Be tender with your spirit.
Hang pictures in your mind of gentle hands.

Let the Dead Bury the Dead

For Tim

   1
You tell me a story:
You were in a monastery in high school
given the job of burying a dead Brother.
You dug the grave and left the casket
balanced on the rim of a hill
while you ran to play ball.
In the late afternoon heat you looked up
saw a dark hole in the blazing sun.
"We forgot to bury Maurillion," you cried
and ran up the hill dropping your bat and ball.
"We forgot to bury Maurillion,"
the old man who died in the light of God.
After that it was a password among you.
"Maurillion" — whenever you started to play
you had to stop and bury him.

   2
I tell you about my dream:
I am lost in time, in the Middle Ages
in Edinburgh.
Kind villagers guide me
around walls of stone
past soldiers' taverns
and the alleys of thieves.
"If I can find the mountain," I say
"I'll be home." I pay them
with meaningless coins, cheap jewelry.
When I knock at the door
children embrace me, but my father
is not glad. It isn't my house anymore.

3

My house
is striped with yellow
trajectories of falling leaves.

My house is falling
is falling

and I rebuild it
almost every day.

My windows take on the open-eyed
stare of a musician playing wholly
for herself. She's testing notes
off the walls to find the shape
of that body she's entered
and accepting the silences
drifting down from the trees.

My house of ribs and skin
a clay bell
begging a little
something
from the wind.

4

Maurillions:
the fear of loving too much
your body smooth to my tongue
your head
that I love to hold
catching your thoughts in my hands
like water.

Early morning, on the mountain
the sun reveals itself slice by slice.
Mist sifts upward into the golden pool
and pines release night's wet treasure
until their outlines are clear.

Then all my Maurillions roll upward
ride on the call of one morning bird.
I am left with now —
this moment.
Without the fear that makes me stop
in the middle of words —
I love you.

Water

look deep
in your cupped hands
you will see me
come to you as water

you know the sea
have absorbed its roar
touched its curves
harvested stones
hidden in the dunes
a long time now

sometimes
I want to call you
but I am frozen
in white country
even the shells
we collected
turn to bone here

some morning
you will touch snow
sifted from my home
or a river that you scoop
as it meets your sea

your hands
will hold me then
as they hold mountains
glaciers, the icicles
we sucked as children

listen
You will hear me
say your name

Cambridge, England 1986
For Tim

An old mill pub
hangs low over the river Cam.

From its walls willow
streamers trail brown water.

I think of you
how you love this slow beauty

the way the cloud
loves its slice of moon.

It swells you the way
history fattens up this lazy river

lives in you
a language that walks your walls.

Today my willow hands
remember the press of you

the earth gone rural
thatched with words that bind us.

I come to hear Romeo woo Juliet
where once we walked green eyed.

I know I would not die for you
but I'd consider it.

From Each Hand

When I walk with my sons
I feel that I am shrinking.

My body once extended two ways
a child hanging from each hand.

Now the mouth of the older one reaches my chin.
He measures me word for word.

The younger fits his head
exactly between my breasts.

They rise beside me   mounds
of the earth I shrink
to meet.

Of Circles and My Sons

"I saw how the planets gathered
like the leaves themselves
Turning in the wind."
                           Wallace Stevens

This poem is for Timmy
for he is onion mouthed.
His words can make me cry.
He describes and catalogues each moment
a geologist examining the ancient hills.
His words like round bodies of birds
hit my windows in October and fly
away without being dazed.
For he winters without me
and returns in spring
growing shadows
only slightly familiar.

This poem is for Andy
for he is radish warm
a flamingo in his cool home.
He runs like a mouse scurrying
his voice a tail dragging behind him.
He swims outward turning his head backward.
He sees earth and flowers
in the frosted winter windows.
His hand fits in mine as a place
where it plans to stay.
He never travels far.

I don't know yet if we are leaves
swirling in a great wind
or the wind itself.
We dance around each other
in ever growing orbits.
We wear each other
like tight rings
impossible to remove.

Oh Yes We Have Been Here Before: Stratford

We walk along the river.
Boats slide lazily between lush green banks.
On the playground children play soccer.
At night we watch Hamlet wrap his death in poetry.

Under thatched roofs we forget
glass cases filled with ragged uniforms
swords with jeweled scabbards
endless lists of names carved in stone.
We forget the news full of America
registering for the draft again.

At home our young sons grow tall
as red pine. Even now an ocean
breaks over their smooth limbs.
The youngest swims for the first time.
Proud, he punches holes in his water wings
then begins to cry.

Something thrown away too soon.

In the North

I buy my son
a small canoe paddle

at night
he comes into my room

it is the paddle
not the water that he needs

I wonder
where he is going

that the paddle
held wide like a wing
can take him?

Letter From a Downtown Hotel

When someone enters a room
in the building across the street
I want to take my clothes off
reenact old movie scenes disturb
the detachment created of height
two layers of dark glass.
Inside another window disembodied
arms and hands pick up a book
leaf through pages write notes
then lift to hold a head.
We couldn't speak if we wanted
only bodies can atone for this
failure.

The western mountains
float in a glass wall.
They point the way I'd run if I could.
At the end of the concrete tunnel
a snow capped peak, solid, rises
in its promise of air and sun.

I could mail them a letter as I
do you but I don't know names.
Dear man who holds his head
propped over a book...
Dear man who is never alone...
I'll send them what I can't send you
a naked body shining at them moving
slowly in front of the window.

I miss you steadily painfully.
Now only an occasional stray pigeon
gets close to my windows
delivering a call from the soft
white flocks of the high country.

White Herons

These white holes
radiate into morning
light collected while we sleep.
One sits frozen on a branch.
The other slow steps across the mulch,
eye on some elusive prey.
The statue raises a claw
to scratch its neck and back.
Slow and easy, only a screaming jay
can rouse those long bodies.
They are like my teenaged boys,
inert but poised in the morning,
faces shining with secrets gathered
during a dark gleaning.

Gifts for a Birthday

Today I ask a gift of the dolphin
to hear music beneath the waves
and many messages at once.
I ask the wind to touch me
with its burden of memory.
I ask to love in the clarity
of moonlight and step away naked.

I am a wheel on the upward swing
into a transit of light.
As I touch ground and rise up again
I ask from the inconstant wind
power to stop the business of survival
to step out of the long line of mothers
grandmothers who made an art of it
to forget the men —bishop, therapist, father
who said, "You can survive anything.
Nothing will destroy you. Expect the worst."

I am no longer a rock washed by the sea.
I ask for more:
the gift of the loon
that swallows the night and flies where it wants
touch of sun that sends me within.
Tonight the spring moon laughs and says,
"It's all right for you to want to stay
always where you are and yet move on."

Growing Older

I am learning
to hold onto the world
learning just in time
that it won't fall
away from me
at night I open my shades
to dry white sounds
mornings I collect
what I can
from surfaces of things
search the bottoms of cups
listen for radiators
one morning I tell you
that I love
to touch your skin
that you are beautiful
when I hold you—
around us waves
of frantic geese
climb the cold

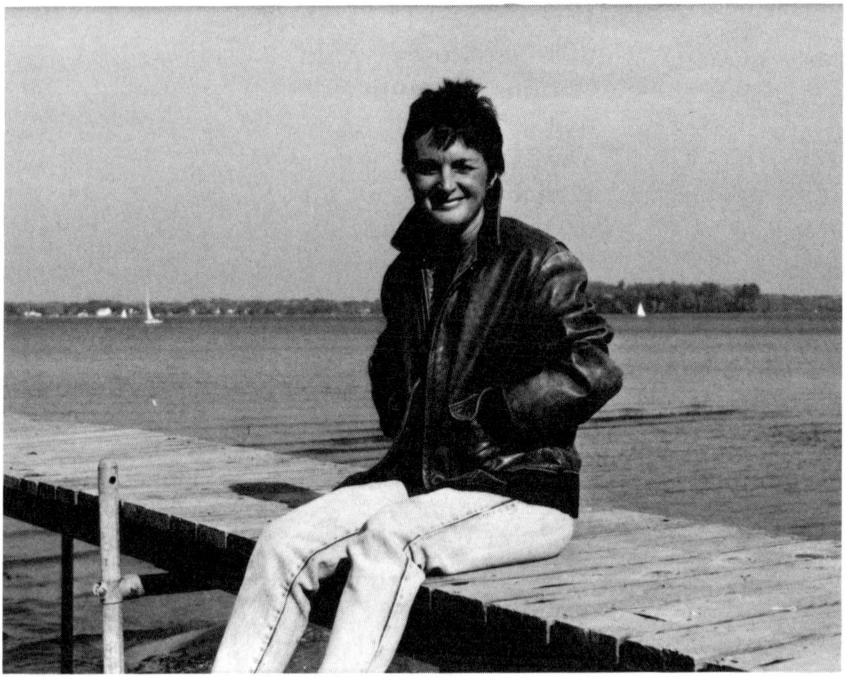

MARY KAY RUMMEL

was born in St. Paul and has lived much of her life in the Twin Cities area. For eight years she was a member of the Sisters of St. Joseph, an experience which is deeply reflected in her poetry She has a Ph.D. in English Education from the University of Minnesota. She teaches at the University of Minnesota and also works for the Compas Writers in the Schools Program and its Dialogue Program. She was a Loft/Mentor winner in 1985-6 and a founding member of Onionskin, a women's poetry collective. She now lives in Fridley, Minnesota with her husband, Tim, and her two sons, Andy and Timothy.

This Body She's Entered documents, lyrically, the powerful metaphysical struggle leading up to Ms. Rummel's decision to leave the religious order, marry, and raise a family. It is at once an affirmation of intense spirituality and womanliness.

"Poetry," she says, "is the spiritual center of my life. Through poetry I name my life, give it meaning and shape. It is the search for the clarifying word that will tie together all the disparate parts of my life. All those roles that are cast out like lines into the air— mother, wife, lover, daughter, sister, writer, teacher, thinker— tangle and twist until my poetry untangles and connects them. My subject matter is anything that gets inside of me, that obsesses me and cries to be let out. Whatever it is it is metaphysical. It has everything to do with being a woman and everything to do with my late discovery that there is no separation between body and spirit. That is why I do it. With poetry there are no endings. It goes on and on. There is always more to do."

This Body She's Entered is Mary Kay Rummel's first book of poems.